YOU LUCKY DOG!

KATE KELLY

D1601497

Cover Credit

Concept: Valerie Jerome

Art: Julie Temple

Photograph Credit

(Bum's picture) San Diego History Center

(Patsy Ann's picture) Derek Reich

ISBN-10: 098921060X
ISBN-13: 978-0-9892106-0-7

DEDICATION AND ACKNOWLEDGMENTS

This book is dedicated to Val Jerome who played two roles in seeing this book through—first in winning over our hearts when she won over the hearts of our dogs, Boo and Lucy.

Her second role—and perhaps the more important in terms of this book—was having the vision for how it should all go together.

Thank you, Val

ABOUT KATE KELLY'S *YOU LUCKY DOG!*

You Lucky Dog! is an uplifting compilation of true stories about homeless dogs that somehow survived and thrived to become local or national celebrities. *You Lucky Dog!* takes us through the historic triumphs of many beloved American dogs, and beautifully recounts the dire adversity each of these amazing creatures faced en route to a grand, serendipitous destiny.

One such story features Bum, a steamship stowaway, St. Bernard mix that, in 1886, disembarked in San Diego. He chose to remain there long enough for the townsfolk to fall in love with him and appoint him the town dog. Despite the efforts by many to adopt him, Bum loved adventure, and refused to stay put. After hopping a northbound freight train, a local San Diego reporter/telegrapher alerted the northern stations en route that San Diego's beloved town dog was aboard, and asked if, upon Bum's arrival, they would show him the local sights then send him home on the next train south, guaranteeing the railroad would pay his passage.

There are many such heartwarming stories in *You Lucky Dog!* that include celebrity dogs, Toto from *The Wizard of Oz*, Benji, and our own top dogs, America's First Dogs. Kate captures their very souls in moving descriptions of the devotion, loyalty and trust that not only changed the fortune of these very special dogs, but also the lives of their human caregivers.

TABLE OF CONTENTS

Part One: Homeless Dogs that Survived and Thrived

TABLE OF CONTENTS - CONTINUED

Part Two: Dogs That Lived at the White House

PART ONE:

HOMELESS DOGS THAT SURVIVED AND THRIVED

BUM, A DOG THAT CHOSE
SAN DIEGO AS HOME

A steamship from San Francisco, the Santa Rosa, arrived in San Diego, and a stowaway disembarked along with some of the other passengers. It was a dog described as a St. Bernard-Spaniel mix that had the good sense to decide that San Diego looked like a good place to settle down.

Someone began calling him "Bum" and the name stuck. He quickly adapted to life on land and made himself a member of the community. At meal times, his primary "go to" place was an establishment run by a Chinese fisherman, Ah Wo Sue. However, Bum was really a dog that wanted to belong to many people. He liked sleeping on the streets and never wanted to go home with anyone particular, perhaps because he knew he would do just fine begging for food at local restaurants and neighborhood butchers. One restaurant capitalized on Bum's appearances by putting up a sign that

1

read, "Bum eats here"–nothing better than an endorsement from the town dog.

Bum thought nothing was more exciting than when the fire bell rang. Along with the volunteer firefighters, Bum was always available to report to a fire.

Bum's Story Documented by a Journalist Who Knew Him

We know as much as we do about Bum's life because James Edward Friend, a journalist and a part-time telegrapher, took time to write about him. Many years later, author William Edward Evans brought these reports to light in the July 1967 *San Diego Historical Society Quarterly*.

One of the stories Friend wrote explained why Bum was missing the lower portion of his right front foreleg. Friend wrote that Bum and a bulldog got into a fight that played out across the train tracks. An oncoming train hit the two dogs; the bulldog was killed and Bum was seriously wounded. When a doctor took a look at Bum, he felt he could save him if he cut off the badly mangled right front paw. Bum eventually healed and was still able to get around San Diego just fine though he sported a somewhat odd three-legged gait.

Another "track story" also involved Bum, this time as a hero. A puppy made his way on to the train tracks, and while journalist James Friend's article did not mention any oncoming threat, Friend gave Bum credit for saving the puppy by getting it off the tracks. Perhaps this is an example of "it's the thought that counts."

Bum, The Traveler

Friend happened to be near the train station one day when he saw Bum attempting to climb aboard a north bound train;

the porter discouraged Bum by turning him around on the steps and pushing him back on to the platform.

Friend notes that "...when the cars began to move away I heard the old dog's well known music. He was lying full length in front of the door, on the rear platform of the rear palace car; thumping the wood with his glad tail, his red tongue hanging from a wide-opened mouth and his sonorous voice telling everybody that he was off for the upper country."

Because Friend was also a telegrapher he stepped into the rail station's telegraph office and sent a message that Bum, San Diego's "town dog," was bound for "Lord knows where." Friend requested that wherever Bum alighted, the people should show him the town and then send him South again...that the train employees would guarantee him free passage.

Friend also sent a direct message to a fellow reporter, Dick Clover, who had worked in San Diego but had more recently moved to the *Los Angeles Herald*. After receiving the telegram about Bum, Clover met the train in L.A., collected Bum and kept him in Los Angeles for a couple of days before sending him back to San Diego.

Greatly Beloved

In 1894 Bum was visiting George Magwood's general store. Magwood was outside putting a halter on a rather nervous horse. Bum got too close to the back of the horse and the dog was kicked; his hind leg was broken. Magwood summoned a doctor and Bum's leg was soon set. The newspaper account mentioned: "Dr. Stone will today take off the bandages and redress the fractured leg. He says Bum will be out and about again in about eight weeks." Readers were told they could stop by and visit Bum at Magwood's any afternoon after 2 p.m.

Bum was never required to have a dog license, but when San Diego passed an ordinance requiring other dogs to have licenses, they knew the perfect dog to depict on the paper document–Bum.

In 1898 Bum was having difficulty getting around because of arthritis so the Board of Supervisors ordered that he be given a home at the County Hospital. He died there on November 19, 1898 and was buried on the grounds.

Memorialized Today: San Diego and Edinburgh

There is a life-size bronze statue of Bum in a pocket park in San Diego in the Gaslamp District just outside the William Heath Davis House, which is now a museum and information center for the Gaslamp District. (The house is the oldest wooden structure in the Gaslamp District. It was a pre-cut saltbox style house that was shipped from the East Coast to San Diego via Cape Horn in 1850.)

Why does Bum continue to fascinate? Recently I contacted Bob Marinaccio, the executive director of the Gaslamp Historical District, to get his opinion. "I think it was Bum's independent spirit," says Marinaccio. "Many of the townspeople would have gladly taken him home, but he wasn't interested. He wanted to belong to the whole community. I think even today people are captured by the idea that the entire town shared this dog."

In 2007 when Bum's statue by artist Jessica McCain was unveiled, the people of San Diego were invited to the ceremony and dog owners were encouraged to bring their dogs.

Beside the statue of Bum sits a statue of another beloved dog, Greyfriar's Bobby. San Diego and Edinburgh town leaders decided to take on "sister city" status because of their two respective town dogs. (Bobby was a Skye terrier who became famous in the 1860s and '70s when the dog insisted on standing watching over his owner's grave in Edinburgh. The dog made his home in the cemetery for 14 years, until he died in 1872.)

San Diego and Edinburgh have matching statues of both dogs, and each year ceremonies are held in the two cities to commemorate the loyalty and love of Bum and Bobby.

If you live in San Diego or are visiting, stop by and give Bum and Bobby a pat. In the fall, the entire family should visit the Gaslamp Quarter when they annually celebrate a "step back in time" festival, featuring hay rides and panning for gold. All activities are representative of the time when Bum would have wandered the streets looking after his people.

KATE KELLY

TOTO/TERRY: THE ROAD TO OZ

The 1939 film of *The Wizard of Oz* is memorable for many reasons, and one of them is certainly the presence of Dorothy's adorable dog, Toto.

How the dog came to be cast in the starring role is a perfect Hollywood story as it involves unkind, deadbeat owners, the rescue of the little dog by a trainer and his family, and of course, it involves little Terry herself, a female

Cairn Terrier, who seemed to understand that succeeding in show business brought with it a guarantee of a good home and never having to go back to her mean owners again.

In the Beginning

But let's back up a bit to explain what happened. Terry is said to have been born in 1933 in Alta Dena, California. She was adopted by a married couple from Pasadena who had no children and evidently no patience for puppy training. Terry had a continuing problem with wetting the rug, and the couple became very frustrated, eventually calling Carl Spitz, who ran the successful Hollywood Dog Training School.

Spitz accepted Terry, and within a relatively short time Terry was housebroken and ready to go home. When Spitz notified the owners, they had no intention of returning for Terry–or paying the bill. As a result, Spitz had acquired a new pup. Spitz lived on the same property where he kept and trained the dogs, and Terry became an occasional guest in the house. It did not take long before she was finding laps to sit in and endearing herself to the family.

The first audition to which Spitz took Terry was one for *Bright Eyes* (1934) starring child star Shirley Temple. After the choice of possible dogs was narrowed down by the casting people, the final test was meeting Shirley and her own dog, a Pomeranian named Ching-Ching. When Terry did well with Ching-Ching, Shirley turned to the adults observing the scene and gave her approval: "She's hired."

The Wizard of Oz

Five additional films followed for Terry. Then Carl Spitz heard that a new film was to be made based on *The Wizard of Oz*. He researched the story and tried to anticipate the type of work the director would expect from a dog; he then ran Terry through training exercises he thought might be appropriate if Terry were cast.

Often when Oz was staged, the part of the dog was either written out or greatly decreased, but when the producers settled on Terry they realized this wasn't necessary. Toto/Terry appears in almost every scene in the movie.

The success of Toto in the film is to Spitz's and Terry's credit. Terry played a part involving a vast cast (think of the Munchkins, the Winkies and the Flying Monkeys) as well as major stars dressed in animal and fantasy costumes. It could not have been easy for a canine to remain cool and collected. Yet Toto mastered everything expected of her–from listening intently when Judy Garland sang *Somewhere over the Rainbow* to withstanding three wind machines mimicking a tornado.

There was, however, one bad incident. A large Winkie accidentally stepped on Terry's foot, and Terry required several days off to recover from the injury.

For her work, Terry was paid $125 per week–more than the Munchkins received.

Toto's performance even merited specific and detailed mention in at least one review. This appeared in *American Girl* Magazine in March 1940:

"The hardest thing this little dog ever had to do was during the drawbridge scene in The Wizard of Oz, when she was chased by the huge Winkie guards of the Wicked Witch. Toto had to come running out of the castle and was trying to cross the drawbridge. She had almost reached the middle [of the bridge] when the drawbridge was pulled straight up. The only safety Toto had was by clutching the edge of the bridge with her little paws and balancing herself thirty feet in the air. One of any dog's greatest fears is the fear of falling, so it took a great deal of courage to follow her master's orders that time."

Terry Becomes Toto Officially

By the end of the film, everyone was calling Terry Toto, and at that point, Spitz decided the only thing to do was to officially change Terry's name. From then on she was known as Toto.

While Toto will always be known for *The Wizard of Oz*, the dog went on to make seven more films. In 1942 Carl Spitz mounted a bus tour for his canine stars to perform and make "personal appearances." In addition to Toto, Spitz took Buck (*Call of the Wild*), Prince Carl (*Wuthering Heights*), Mr. Binkie (*The Light that Failed*), and Musty (*Swiss Family Robinson*).

Toto's last film came out in 1945 and Toto was getting ready to retire by that time. She lived comfortably in the Spitz household until the autumn of 1945 when she died. The Spitz family buried him in their backyard, never thinking that one day they would have to move.

In 1958 the Ventura Freeway was being built near the land where the Spitz's home and kennel were located, and the family was forced to find a new location, eventually buying a kennel property that belonged to Rudd Weatherwax (trainer of Lassie). The Hollywood Dog Training School, created by Carl Spitz and sold to current owner Rick Karl, is still on Vanowen in north Hollywood at the current location. The family moved, but had to leave behind Toto and the remains of other dogs buried in their pet cemetery.

Hollywood Forever

Today, however, there is a place to visit and remember Toto. In 2011 a memorial at the Hollywood Forever Cemetery, funded by an active group of Toto fans, was unveiled in memory of Toto.

A dog's life is not always easy to research but writer and director Willard Carroll (1955-) was determined to track down everything he could and has put together Toto's story by writing Toto's autobiography in the dog's voice. The facts are what you read above but the voice Carroll creates for the canine star is quite amusing. (Information on the book is in the Resources section.)

OWNEY:
OWNED THE ALBANY POST OFFICE

The time was winter 1886, and the place was the post office in Albany, New York, where a cold, bedraggled fox terrier made his way inside looking for shelter.

The postal clerks took him in, fed him, and provided the dog with a warm place to sleep. Owney, as they called him, felt right at home and decided it was his job to follow the mail wagons from the post office to the rail station and back again.

One day he slipped on to a rail car, and several days later he caught another train back to Albany. Owney began to travel regularly, probably encouraged by some humans, but he always returned to the home office. The clerks in Albany were fond of him and were worried about losing him, so they gave him a collar with the inscription, "Owney, Albany P.O., N.Y."

For eleven years, Owney traveled throughout the United States, from New York to California, and he had the tags to prove it. Other post offices began tagging him with "postmarks" that specified where he had visited. Miners in the West inscribed some molded silver as a label of his visit to a mining community; others labeled him with tags of leather or scraps of cloth. Owney started each trip fresh, because in Albany his friends removed and preserved the tags from his previous trip. Occasionally a "travel" book was sent along with him to further document his trips.

On one occasion he hopped the mail train to Montreal, but when he arrived at the Montreal Post Office, after escorting the mail there, he was seized by the Montreal police because he didn't have a dog license. His friends at the Albany Post Office bailed him out by paying for the license, and he was soon on a mail train back to Albany.

In July of 1894 a report in *The New Orleans Times-Democrat* noted that Owney was back in New Orleans again. His last visit to the city had been in the winter of 1892. The article notes: "He never travels in any but mail cars, and when he reaches a town that he forms a good opinion of from the car door, he follows the mail wagon to the Post Office, and when he is ready to travel again, he follows the wagon to some train and is off for parts unknown. Since he was here, Owney has taken in the World's Fair and a part of the widespread labor troubles…[traveling] to Seattle, Washington, Kansas City, Mo.; Memphis, Fort Worth, Taylor, Texas; Waco, San Antonio and Houston."

Eventually Owney traveled internationally. One of his medals documented an audience with the prime minster of Japan. Owney had become quite a celebrity.

Today Owney's body has been stuffed and preserved and stands guard in a glass case in Washington, D.C., serving as a reminder of the importance of goodness and loyalty. (*New York Times*, 3-20-1910)

On July 27, 2011 the postal service released a commemorative stamp in Owney's honor.

KATE KELLY

DORSEY:
A DOG THAT DELIVERED THE MAIL

In the 1880s the people of Calico, California (northeast of Los Angeles) had an unusual mail carrier—a dog.

Jim Stacy worked as postmaster in Calico and his brother Alwin ran a general store near the Bismarck mines, about a mile and half from Calico.

At some point, Jim Stacy acquired a dog named Dorsey. Dorsey has been identified as a Border Collie, an English Shepherd and a Scotch Collie, but more likely was some mixture of any of the above. The story goes that one day Jim wanted to get a message to Alwin but didn't want to make the trip himself. He decided to experiment by tying a letter around Dorsey's neck. He took the dog out and pointed him toward the other town, saying "Bismarck!"

Dorsey hesitated at first but with added encouragement he started on his trip. Dorsey was not seen around Calico the rest of the day but the next day he appeared with a response from Alwin.

The idea of Dorsey carrying a letter or two back and forth soon caught on with the miners who loved the Dog Delivery System. At first, Dorsey was sent off with just a couple of letters that could be tied to his collar, but then one of the Stacy brothers came up with a way to create a wearable mail pouch for the dog. Soon Dorsey's route became a regular thing. The miners reported that Dorsey stopped at one or two of their houses where he was petted and likely fed, but he concluded his trip by stopping off at the store where the pouch was unloaded and reloaded with outgoing messages.

From 1883-1886 Dorsey regularly carried the U.S. mail. The assignment ended only because the mine closed and many of the miners moved away. When the Stacy brothers moved to a new community it was said that they gave Dorsey to San Francisco financier John S. Doe, who owned an interest in the mine.

The story of Dorsey was given added life when country western singer Kenny Rogers recorded an album called *The Ballad of Calico* in 1972. One of the songs was called "Dorsey, the Mail Carrying Dog."

PATSY ANN:
JUNEAU'S VIGILANT HARBOR MASTER

Patsy Ann was a bull terrier who was born deaf on October 12, 1929, according to information provided by the Friends of Patsy Ann. As a pup, she was brought from Portland, Oregon to Juneau where she lived the rest of her life.

While very much a permanent resident of Juneau, she never had a permanent address. She visited the shops and bars and restaurants where owners and patrons were happy to slip her a bite to eat.

Official Greeter

Despite her deafness, Patsy Ann had an unerring sense of the arrival of incoming ships. Perhaps the ships' whistles were at a pitch that permitted her to hear them? At any rate, somehow she sensed their arrival. Whenever a ship was coming into port, Patsy Ann was at the dock in advance and was ready to welcome all comers.

A website created by the Friends of Patsy Ann tells that one day residents had been told a ship would be arriving at one particular dock; Patsy Ann saw the crowd, paused for a moment, and then turned and went to wait at a different dock–the one where the ship actually pulled in.

Most nights Patsy Ann would make her way to the longshoreman's hall where they were happy to have her bed down for the night.

As Patsy aged, she suffered from arthritis that was complicated by her expanding waistline due to being fed by many. Despite any infirmities, she still managed to be at the docks whenever a ship arrived.

On March 30, 1942, she died peacefully at the longshoreman's hall. The next day a crowd of townspeople gathered to say good-bye as her coffin was lowered into the water in the channel over which she had kept close watch for so many years.

Sculpture Commissioned

Fifty years later (1992), the Friends of Patsy Ann held a competition for a sculptor and commissioned Anna Burke Harris to sculpt an "on watch" version of Patsy Ann. The photo above is a picture of Patsy Ann as the statue has been placed, looking out over the water and continuing to greet all who visit Juneau. (Thanks to Derek Reich for permission to use the photo.)

SINBAD: COAST GUARD MASCOT

The story goes that in 1937 two Coast Guardsmen were returning to their ship, *The U.S.S. George W. Campbell*, that was docked in Staten Island. That night they carried with them a bag they were trying to conceal. Once in their bunk they opened the bag to reveal to some of the other men a black and tan mutt with white eyebrows. The pup was quiet that night but the next morning his barking announced to all that a new sailor had come on board.

He was soon named Sinbad. From 1937-1948 he was a member of the crew on the *Campbell*. More than a mascot, Sinbad was a full member of the Coast Guard. He had his own service number, bunk, a uniform of sorts, and an assigned battle station. The men relied on Sinbad for morale and for fun. No one could be bored if Sinbad was around.

In April of 1943 Sinbad was mentioned in *The New York Times* (April 6, 1943) when the *Campbell* was in port where a number of its crew were receiving awards for their anti-submarine patrol work. Commander James A. Hirshfield talked about the fact that Coast Guard cutters were being effectively used for the difficult and dangerous job of ramming enemy submarines. In February the Campbell had battled six enemy submarines over a 12-hour period, sinking at least one of them.

Hirshfield noted to the reporter that the sailors had a superstition that as long as Sinbad was on board nothing would happen to the *Campbell*.

A Sailor with Flaws—and Paws

Like most sailors, Sinbad was not perfect. As described by Eddie Lloyd, editor of the old Coast Guard magazine: "Sinbad was a salty sailor but he's not a good sailor. He'll never rate gold hash marks nor good conduct medals. He's been on report several times, and he's raised hell in a number of ports. On a few occasions, he has embarrassed the United States government by creating disturbances in foreign zones. Perhaps that's why Coast Guardsmen love Sinbad—He's as bad as the worst and as good as the best of us."

In 1946 the George W. Campbell was docked in Charleston for repairs so Sinbad was scheduled for his first official peacetime visit to New York City. He had become quite a celebrity by this time, so when he arrived at

Pennsylvania Station, a 24-piece Coast Guard District Band welcomed him. He then was taken to City Hall and was given a jeep parade to Coast Guard Headquarters where *The New York Times* reported Sinbad was expected to hold a "press conference." He was also scheduled to meet with Coast Guard commandant Admiral Joseph Farley before the screening of two Coast guard films at the Museum of Modern Art. Sinbad, however, was a no-show. One of the officers told the Times that "he was exhausted." (*New York Times*, January 9, 1946).

By 1948, Sinbad was slowing down; he received an honorable discharge because the Coast Guard decided to discount his two Court Martials. He spent the remaining years of his life at Barnegat Coast Guard Station in New Jersey. He died on December 30, 1951. The Resources section will direct you to more stories of Coast Guard mascots.

KATE KELLY

BOOTS TO SINBAD:
DOG-TO-DOG LETTERS

When I originally wrote about Sinbad, I received an email from Coast Guard historian Mike Walling, who has written a great deal about the Coast Guard and the Navy and has collected many personal stories from veterans from World War II, Korea, Viet Nam and Iraq. He has also published a book about Sinbad so he had additional information to share.

In his research, Mike had come upon two letters that appeared in the *USS Campbell Newsletter*, October 11, 1943. He was kind enough to send them on to me. One is a letter written to Sinbad from Boots, a dog who was still stateside. The second letter was Sinbad's reply. Walling writes: "To the best of my knowledge, it is the only letter that Sinbad received along with a copy of his reply that survived World War II."

These letters–written as if the dogs are writing to one another–are so touching. In reading them, you can't help but come away with a better understanding of the sacrifice of war.

Aug. 18, 1943
Sinbad, Mascot,
c/o Postmaster, New York

Dear Sinbad,

We read about you and saw your picture in a magazine. Mom said to me, "Mr. Boots, he's just like you. He must be your twin. We must send him your picture." So Mom took my picture and here it is.

Say, boy, you really must rate on that ship, since you are the only man on board whom the captain cites and calls by name. But, boy, does it burn me up. You see, our Bud went off on his ship right after Pearl Harbor and I begged so hard to go, but he just patted my head and said, "'You can't go, Mr. Boots. You stay here and take care of Mom.' I must settle."

Then he said, "Besides, there's no room on a battleship for a little fellow like you." No room on Battleship X for me! Say, boy, your ship must be much bigger than a battleship, for they took you on and you are five pounds bigger'n me.

Mom says I'm bench-legged. What's bench-legged? I'm black and tan and white with dark brown eyes, and Mom says I'm barrel chested just like you. What's barrel chested,

Sinbad? Mom says she loved your story and suspects you're a reprobate, a rounder and a seasoned old salt, pickled in alcohol. Are you? And she says, "But, Mr. Boots, you're a refined little gent'man, a landlubber, and your morals are above Sinbad's. What's morals?

What I'm writing is a military secret between you and me. I cross my heart and swear I'll never tell if you do what I ask. You see, Mom and I want to know something about Bud. When you are sailing the seas in your big ship, keep a sharp lookout for Battleship X, because Bud is gunnery officer on her. You will recognize him because nobody else on earth looks like Bud or smiles like him. He will smile at you, for he smiles at all little dogs, and you will know it's Bud.

They call him "Corky" in the Navy, so keep your ears cocked, and if you should see him, will you, Sinbad, let me know? I will die a martyr before I tell our secret.

Your twin in the service,

Boots Ward

Sinbad Writes to Mr. Boots

At sea (to you)
At home (to me)

Oct. 11, 1943.
Dear Mr. Boots–
Say, that was such a nice letter you wrote to me and I do appreciate your kindness and thoughtfulness. It is a pleasure to know you for your life story is interesting to me just as mine has been made interesting to other people. Secretly, though, Mr. Boots, I'm just a plain ole dog who has more honest-to-goodness real friends than anyone I ever heard of, and to me that's what really counts…

You're real lucky to have Mom and Bud. You see, I don't know where I came from except that I'm told I was just a puppy when I came to this ship six years ago. …Now, sailors are the hardest working, most patriotic and fun loving men in the world. We get on the beach and due to the strong salt air we have inhaled constantly for weeks on end; naturally we want something to quench our thirst. A few beers are tasty and I, like my buddies, enjoy them immensely.

Concerning my morals, I would say they are good, Mr. Boots, because I have a slant on life that is probably a little different from your viewpoint. My life, as I see it, is for a group of hard fighting, hard working men doing everything in their power to the extent of sacrificing their lives to bring peace and unity to this world. My work is to keep up their spirits, to keep smiles on their faces, their hearts light and carefree. It's a big job to work for more than 200 men–real American men.

If I should ever run into Bud Ward, I'll surely tell him I'm your friend. I'll bet he'll pat me and hug me around the neck, but I know what he'll be thinking. He'll be hugging me because he misses you so much. That, Mr. Boots, is another one my jobs. The boys out here have left their best friends behind, just like Mr. Bud did, so I try to squeeze into a little corner of the empty space in their hearts. Most people say I'm an enlisted man's dog. I consider the officers my good friends too, but they don't take as much time to play with me and I feel much more carefree with the men and I never make a mess where it caused any trouble. So you can see that I am surrounded by enlisted men practically all the time.

During action, of which we have had aplenty, the terrific noise of the guns and explosives bothers me quite a bit. Not that I'm scared, because I know that my buddies have trained their hearts out and will take care of our ship. But I'm afraid sometimes, just worried sick over what might happen to some of them. I usually get in one of the boys' bunks and place my paws over my ears to help protect them from the noise. After everything quiets down, I come up on the topsides prancing and barking to bring my buddies' feelings back to normal quickly.

I can't bark worth a darn, Mr. Boots, can you? I suppose it must be the sea life I've led. I have been in a number of countries and have coins from every one of them on my collar. I am sending you some for your collar. I have been north of the Arctic Circle and the certificate proving the fact hangs in our Mess Deck. I am an honorary member of the Veterans of Foreign Wars, with papers duly signed and sealed at an Army camp on the fighting front. See how swell people have treated me? That's why I do all I can for them.

In closing, I'll let you in on a secret just between you and me and my buddies on the ship because I don't want it spread around. You know how the boys like to nickname each other? Well, instead of calling me Sinbad all the time they sometimes call me "Stinky" but I just ignore them and pass it off with a shrug!

It has been fun talking to you and Mom, Mr. Boots. Keep your chin up and do all you can to take care of Mom until that happy day when Mr. Bud will come smiling home. In the meantime I must do my daily work. Until we meet when you share my bone, if you care to…

Best of luck,
Sinbad
Dog 1/C USCG

[NOTE: Sinbad's letter was signed by his own footprint and it was mailed to "Boots" Ward – Sinbad's twin.]

BENJI,
SHELTER DOG TURNED MOVIE STAR

The lovable mixed-breed dog that was to become Benji was discovered in 1960 by veteran Hollywood animal trainer Frank Inn (1916-2002). Inn always looked first at shelters for the animals he needed for various show requests. The Burbank Animal Shelter was where he found and fell in love with the shaggy brown dog, known as Higgins, that was to be his biggest star.

Who Was Frank Inn?

Inn was born to a Quaker family in Camby, Indiana, and his original name was Elias Franklin Freeman. He left home at age 17, intent on making a name for himself in

Hollywood. Two years later he was seriously injured in a car accident and was convalescing at a friend's house at a time when the family dog had just had a litter of pups. Frank discovered he had a knack for working with animals. His ability soon landed him a job with Rudd Weatherwax, who trained Lassie and Rin-Tin-Tin.

After 14 years working for Weatherwax, Inn went into business for himself and moved his family to an isolated area in the San Fernando Valley to accommodate his growing menagerie of more than 100 dogs, cats and exotic animals. A few years after going on his own, Frank Inn acquired Higgins.

Higgins, who eventually starred as Benji, was originally seen on television as the nameless dog in Petticoat Junction. Inn noted that Higgins successfully mastered a new trick each week for the television show, and his looks and ability made him a natural for a bigger role.

Benji, the Movie

When the movie, Benji, was being cast, there were few signs that it would be a big success. The idea for the film came from Joe Camp, a fellow who made his living producing commercials in Dallas. Camp wrote the script, and began contacting people in Hollywood, only to receive rejection after rejection.

Camp was not going to be discouraged; he still loved his "dog picture " idea. In 1971 Camp and a partner decided to produce the movie independently and then try to get a distribution deal. That, too, proved to be an unreachable goal; Camp and his partner formed their own distribution company and released the picture themselves from their offices in Dallas. Camp personally developed the marketing strategy, wrote the advertising copy and press releases, and supervised each and every booking worldwide.

In spite of the many obstacles to getting the film made, the audiences loved *Benji*. Variety reported the picture was the #3 grossing movie of the year.

Success Equals Sequel

The success of the movie led to a sequel, but by this time Higgins, who was 14 at the time the original movie was filmed, was now too old for a full-time commitment. Higgins' daughter, Benjean, played Benji in *For the Love of Benji* (1977). When the time came for a third Benji, another of Higgins' offspring filled in.

In 2002 Joe Camp was contemplating another *Benji* feature film; Frank Inn had just passed away, so Camp decided the thing to do was to undertake a nationwide shelter search for a new Benji. The publicity would be good for the brand, and in the 1970s the Humane Society had attributed a million additional adoptions to the news that the original Benji had come from a shelter. Camp thought this was a great opportunity to draw attention to the millions of abandoned dogs in shelters nationwide.

Joe Camp and his company undertook a nationwide search, looking at animals from Los Angeles and Detroit to points east and south. The field was narrowed to three candidates that were then put through a "Benji boot camp" run by Camp's wife. Ultimately, the new Benji was a dog from a shelter in Gulfport, Mississippi. The runners-up were taken care of, too. One was placed with a family, and the other was cast as Benji's sidekick in the film, *Benji, Off the Leash*.

Benji reminds us that anyone thinking of adopting a new pet, should remember to check with local shelters.

KATE KELLY

SHEP,
FAITHFUL DOG OF MONTANA

If you have ever visited Fort Benton, Montana, then you have seen the monument to "Faithful Shep" that sits above the river alongside the train tracks.

The most often-told version of the story notes that in 1936 a dog was first noticed at the Great Northern Railway station in Fort Benton one day when a casket was being loaded on to a train going east from Montana. The dog kept greeting incoming trains for years afterward.

In the late 1930s, conductor Ed Shields pieced together more details of the story, and more recently, Fort Benton historian Ken Robison has written about it, making the story much more understandable. Robison writes that the dog was first spotted outside St. Clare Hospital in Fort Benton; an ailing shepherd had come in for care earlier in the day. The shepherd did not live long, and his family requested the body be sent east to them. A nun arranged for the casket to be picked up and taken to the train.

Robison reports that people noted that a dog watched as the body left the hospital, and he followed the truck carrying the casket to the train. When the casket was placed inside the rail car, the dog whined and pawed at the door.

The Vigil Begins

The dog remained at the station, sleeping under benches most of the time but coming out each time a train pulled in. Only over time did he begin to warm to the station employees; they fed him and watched out for him, calling him "Shep" since he was clearly a herding dog. Shep actually became quite famous and was even mentioned in *Ripley's Believe It or Not* column. Though there were offers from people all over the country who wanted to adopt Shep, the station employees knew that the dog wanted to remain at the station on his vigil.

Shep grew older, and on January 12, 1942, Shep did not seem to hear an oncoming train. The engineer saw the dog on the track but was unable to stop, or Shep may have slipped on ice or snow in trying to get off the rails in time.

Shep's funeral was held two days later, and the entire town was said to have come to honor Shep. Pall bearer duties were split between station employees and several boy scouts. Shep was buried on the bluff overlooking the station.

Shortly after Shep's death, Ed Shields, the conductor who uncovered details to tell the story, began to sell a booklet about the faithful dog. He wanted something good to come as a result of the dog's unwavering loyalty to his original owner.

Fort Benton was the location of a Montana School for the Deaf and Blind, and Shields decided that supporting this local school was a fitting way to use the funds earned from the booklet. People were also invited to donate money in Shep's honor; it is estimated that the Shep fund had brought in over $100,000.

I called the school recently, and the fund is still active. Donations in memory of Shep can be made to:

Montana School for the Deaf and Blind
3911 Central Avenue
Great Falls, MT 59405

In memory of the 50th anniversary since Shep's accident, the town commissioned a bronze sculpture of Shep. Today it sits on the bank of the Missouri River, near the train tracks. A historical marker tells of Shep's vigil. Boy Scout Troop 47 still cares for Shep's memorial and grave site.

KATE KELLY

THE TRUE STORY OF RIN-TIN-TIN

Like most Hollywood legends, the story of Rin-Tin-Tin has many versions. From the beginning Rin-Tin-Tin's owner and trainer, Lee Duncan, who did not come from any type of show business background, knew the importance of "story" and all the studio had to do was pick up on the story line Duncan created.

Duncan (1893-1960) was born into a poor family in California. His father soon left them, and in 1898, his mother placed Lee and his sister in an orphanage as she was unable to support and take care of them. (Orphanages were sometimes used for temporary placements at this time.)

By 1900 Lee and his sister were with their mother again, living with an uncle. As explained by researcher and author Ann Elwood in her excellent book, *Rin-Tin-Tin The Movie Star*, this aspect of Duncan's background helps explain

Duncan's allegiance to his dogs at the expense of human relationships, a trait that is consistent throughout Duncan's life and probably contributed to his undivided devotion to building Rin-Tin-Tin's career.

Duncan Acquires the Dog in Europe

While the birth of Rin-Tin-Tin in Germany and the adoption of Rinty and his sister Nanette is undisputed, the story that the pups were found on a battlefield is likely untrue, according to Elwood who tracked back through war timelines as well as the movements of Duncan's squadron at the time. Based on the age of the dog, Elwood makes a compelling case for the belief that an older dog was found by the soldiers and this dog mated with a local dog to produce the puppies in question.

At any rate, Duncan totally devoted himself to being with the dogs rather than his fellow soldiers. Given the young age of the pups, it would have been a major time commitment. The story of "found on the battlefield" amidst a hail of gunfire was the story Duncan came home and told, and it certainly suited the studio press office.

When the fighting ended and troops were coming back to the U.S., Duncan was not leaving without his pups, and he convinced a superior to help him get permission to bring back Rinty and Nanette. (Nanette became ill on the journey to the States and eventually died of distemper.) Rin-Tin-Tin and Duncan made it all the way back to California where Duncan returned to a job at a high end sporting goods store where the owner frequently arranged hunting trips for his wealthy clients. Duncan, who had worked with hunting dogs before the war, became one of the regular guides. This may have given him social connections to the well-to-do of

Hollywood that eventually helped Rin-Tin-Tin step into movie stardom.

Well-Trained and Talented

One thing about which there is no doubt is that Rin-Tin-Tin was a handsome and well-trained dog who was capable of great athleticism.

Rin-Tin-Tin first came to public notice at a dog show in Los Angeles where he performed some of the feats he and Duncan had been working on, including the scaling of an 11-foot, 9-inch wall.

Between the dog's very notable talents and Duncan's ability to connect with the right people, Rin-Tin-Tin had his first movie part in *The Man From Hell's River*, and his career blossomed from there. Eventually Rinty made 26 films for Warner Brothers.

Another myth of the day was that Rin-Tin-Tin saved Warner Studios from financial ruin. In her book, Elwood gives full due to Rin-Tin-Tin's box office success for Warner Brothers but does not fully buy into the "saved the studio" myth.

Not unlike other movie stars of his day, Rin-Tin-Tin was caught in a studio system where his living circumstances were determined by the requirements of his contract and by those who provided insurance for the star's well-being. The famous dog lived in a kennel, it seems, because Duncan believed that was best for him, but the studio's insurers placed other restrictions. Because they did not want him to roam free where he might get hurt, his exercise had to be taken at scheduled intervals on a hamster-wheel type of device.

While other dog stars eventually retired to a cottage with their trainer or some other loving soul, Duncan kept both

Rinty and himself on task at all times. When not busy filming, Duncan put them on the road where they performed several times a day as part of various vaudeville shows, or he took Rinty to animal shelters and orphanages to provide awareness of some of the social issues Duncan clearly cared about. No matter what, Rin-Tin-Tin spent almost all of his days working.

Rin-Tin-Tin may at some point have been affected by the stress. The press reported on one occasion that doing too many "re-takes" may have caused Rin-Tin-Tin to take a nip out of one of his stars. Another time it was reported that he turned a pretend fight into an all-too-real tussle.

Based on Elwood's detailed and well-substantiated research, it seems clear that one of the best known dogs in show business was just like his contemporary human counterparts who were victims of the "studio system," trapped in a moneymaking scenario over which he had no control.

The career of the original Rin-Tin-Tin outlasted the coming of the talkies, and while dog pictures became less popular in the early 1930s, Rinty was still performing in 1931. Duncan was accepting deals for 1932 when Rinty died somewhat unexpectedly of what would have been some age-related ailment.

Later, Duncan kept his career going with Rin-Tin-Tin Junior who was the first of a long line of offspring to continue the family tradition.

Duncan did not pass away until 1960 but in 1957 he accepted a proposal from Jannettia Brodsgaard Propps who had been begging him for a puppy for a year so that she could continue the lineage. Her kennel, Bodyguard Kennels, eventually got a puppy, and she was careful to consult Duncan about genetic preferences he wanted for the line; it was she who successfully maintained the next generations of

Rin-Tin-Tin offspring. When she died in 1988, her granddaughter, Daphne Hereford, took over the kennel; the dogs produced today are as similar as possible in structure, color, and intelligence to the original Rin-Tin-Tin who began it all.

SERGEANT STUBBY
(1916 OR 1917-MARCH 16, 1926),
WORLD WAR I MASCOT

Though the United States did not yet have an official program for using dogs in the military until World War II, one dog–a pit bull–earned a place in the infantry during World War I and was responsible for saving many lives. Those who own pit bulls say that loyalty is a strong trait within the breed, and Stubby's loyalty to his men meant that he came home a hero and the mascot of World War I.

Corporal Robert Conroy was completing military training near the Yale Bowl in New Haven, Connecticut when he came upon a stray pup that kept showing up at the men's drill practices. Whether Conroy called him Stubby because of his short tail or his chunky body is unclear, but Stubby was friendly and remained a constant presence wherever the

102nd Infantry (part of the Army's 26th Division) was practicing their drills.

When the unit was to be moved to Newport News, Virginia, Conroy hid Stubby in some of the equipment so that he could go with them. From there they were to be shipped overseas, so Corporal Conroy found an open-minded military policeman who helped him find a place on the ship for Stubby so he could come to France with the men.

Stubby spent the next year and a half on the front line, participating in seventeen battles, including those at Chateau-Thierry, the Marne, and Saint-Mihiel. His acute sense of hearing and smell were invaluable to the men. He could hear the high-pitched whine of the shells before the soldiers did, so the men took to watching Stubby to see if he had noted anything. Another night Stubby smelled gas, and he went running through the trenches to wake the men; Stubby breathed in enough gas that Conroy had to take him to the base hospital to be revived. Conroy tried to develop a gas mask for Stubby but it was hard to get anything that fit around his flat nose. (During WWII, the United States began issuing gas masks for dogs.)

On another occasion, Stubby awakened Conroy. Conroy grabbed his gun and followed Stubby outside where he found that a German soldier had infiltrated the American line. Stubby moved forward and sunk his teeth into the fellow's leg. With this distraction, Conroy got the upper hand with the German and was able to arrest him. Stubby, however, wasn't certain his job was done–it took some coaxing to get him to let go of the man's leg.

While in the Toul area, Stubby was nearby when a grenade exploded, and the dog was hit. Again, Conroy took Stubby for medical care, and six weeks later Stubby returned to be where he belonged–with his unit.

Over time, word got out about this brave dog that was loyal under fire and willing to risk all for his men. The people of France were first-hand observers; some French women made a coat for Stubby out of a U.S. Army blanket, and people began pinning medals to it. As the story of Stubby's loyalty and heroism became known, it was both comforting and inspirational.

Back in the U.S.

When Conroy and Stubby returned to the United States in 1919, the dog was highly sought after. He was honored by the Humane Society, the American Red Cross, and the American Legion. The YMCA gave Stubby a membership card promising "three bones a day and a place to sleep." Stubby led many parades and appeared in photos with several presidents–Wilson, Harding, and Coolidge all had their pictures taken with Stubby.

Robert Conroy enrolled in Georgetown Law School in 1921, and Stubby became mascot of the football team. The crowds loved seeing him on the field.

Stubby died of old age in 1926, and Conroy held him in his arms until the dog had taken his last breath.

His tombstone read: "Sergeant Stubby, Hero Dog of WWI a Brave Stray." As recently as 2006, Stubby was honored as part of a World War I monument in Kansas City. Anyone who visits can find a brick in memory of Stubby along the Walk of Honor.

KATE KELLY

BUD:
FIRST DOG TO CROSS U.S. BY AUTO

In 2003 Ken Burns released a delightful documentary, *Horatio's Drive*, telling the story of the very first cross-country trip by automobile. The trip was undertaken in 1903 by a Vermont doctor, Horatio Nelson Jackson, who agreed to attempt it in order to win a $50 bet. Along the way he acquired a dog Bud that made the trip as well.

Jackson and his wife were in San Francisco because Jackson was recovering from health problems and could not spend the winter in Vermont. On May 18, Horatio Jackson was having a drink at the San Francisco University Club when he got into a discussion about the future of automobiles. Most people felt they were a useless fad but Jackson believed they were the next big thing. He accepted the other men's challenge: to be the first to travel cross-country by automobile. The wager placed was $50 (about $1200 today).

The terms specified that Jackson could travel with a mechanic, and he selected a 22-year-old fellow named Sewall Crocker who was given the job of choosing the car. Crocker selected a twenty-horsepower, two-cylinder automobile made by the Winton Motor Carriage Company. Jackson purchased the supplies they would need which included fishing gear, pots, pans, and sleeping bags as well as assorted items for keeping the car going through what promised to be challenging terrain. Jackson provided an ax, a spade, extra tools, a pistol, and spare containers for water and gas...there were no gas stations along the route as there was not yet a route at all. They had a few basic maps of some areas that had been used by cyclists, but otherwise they planned to prevail on the kindness of strangers to point the way.

Fifteen miles into the trip, the car blew a tire—the first of many mishaps. Just outside Sacramento they lost all their cooking gear when it fell off the back of the car without them even noticing. The trip proceeded with many similar challenges—getting gas or fixing a tire often became a major ordeal.

In addition, people were so excited to see the travelers that some of them would purposely tell them a route that took them out of the adventurers' way but directly into the path of friends or relatives of the person giving directions.

A Dog

The story goes that Dr. Jackson had originally wanted a dog to go along with him but he had not yet gotten one before their departure on May 23. They were in Idaho and had stayed in a hotel in Caldwell. A few miles out of town,

Jackson realized he forgot his coat so, according to the PBS website, they turned around. On their way back to Caldwell, a man offered to sell them a bull terrier pup for $15. Jackson accepted the offer; they named the dog Bud, and Bud became a big attraction everywhere they went.

Cars were totally open in that day, so road dirt and dust flew directly at the passengers all day long. When it became clear that Bud's eyes were as irritated by the dust as the men's would have been without goggles, Dr. Jackson took a pair of goggles and fit them to Bud's head. He wore them the rest of the trip.

Part of the challenge of the original bet involved making the trip in fewer than 90 days, and this caught the interest of car manufacturers. Soon a team of men driving a Packard and another group driving an Oldsmobile were trying to keep up with Jackson and win what they had turned into a cross-country race.

But Bud, Sewall Crocker, and Horatio Jackson were the victors. They had averaged 71 miles per day, and they drove down Fifth Avenue in New York City at 4 a.m. on July 26, 1903. Jackson claimed his $50 winnings and noted that it had cost him about $8000–for car, parts, food, lodging, 800 gallons of gas–to win the bet.

Bud had been the perfect companion. He had become quite skilled at watching the road and bracing for hills and bumps, and Jackson noted that was the only member of the trio who "used no profanity for the entire trip."

Epilogue

Bud was perfectly happy to trade in his life on the road for retirement at Jackson's home in Vermont with occasional car trips into Burlington. Crocker eventually got sponsored to do a two-year auto tour of Europe. Jackson used his fame to become a successful businessman in Vermont, and his health must have improved as he eventually enlisted to be among the older men fighting in World War I.

And Dr. Jackson and Mrs. Jackson seemed to have lived contentedly in Vermont with only one driving incident to mar their memories. One day in Burlington, Jackson got ticketed for speeding—he was going over 6 miles per hour. No word as to whether Bud was along to witness the humiliation.

SALLIE, CIVIL WAR MASCOT

In 1861 the captain of the brand new Pennsylvania infantry unit (the 11th Volunteer Infantry) was busy training his regiment in West Chester, Pennsylvania, when a townsperson presented him with a four-to-five week old puppy, a bull terrier.

With so many possible people to play with him and feed him, the puppy was quickly absorbed as part of the unit. The men named her after one of the more beautiful young ladies who had caught their attention in West Chester. Sallie was fed and played with during the weeks and months that followed, and when she heard the sound of reveille, she came immediately, always among the first for roll call.

Sallie's first battle was at Cedar Mountain in 1862. It was reported that she remained right with the color guard throughout the entire battle. She continued this pattern of staying with the front line at Antietam, Fredericksburg, and Chancellorsville. The soldiers reported that she raced around and barked at the enemy, providing moral support and inspiration to the men.

At Gettysburg, Sallie was separated from her unit when the men fell back during the first day of fighting. She returned to the field where the regiment had started and waited with those who had fallen there.

After the Confederate retreat, a soldier from a Massachusetts unit found her on the field and recognized that she was the dog that accompanied the Pennsylvania infantry. He returned her to her regiment.

In May of 1863 she was wounded at Spotsylvania but one of the men patched up her neck and she stayed with the unit. At Hatcher's Run (February 1865), Sallie's luck ran out. She moved forward with the first line of men and was shot and died instantly. As the second line moved through, they found her body. The soldiers, many of them weeping, buried Sallie in the field where they found her.

In 1890, survivors from the 11th Pennsylvania Infantry dedicated a monument at Gettysburg. The monument shows a vigilant soldier, standing watch. At the base of the statue is a bronze likeness of a dog...it is Sallie.

If you visit Gettysburg, be sure to stop at this monument on Oak Ridge. People who drive by too quickly will miss the statue of the loyal little dog who gave her life in order to be true to her unit. And if you stop, you'll probably find that previous visitors have left dog biscuits right by Sallie, in her honor.

SHANDA, THE DOG MAYOR:
STORY STOLEN BY A CAT

When looking for amazing stories about dogs, I came upon Shanda, a golden retriever, who served as mayor of Guffey, Colorado from 1993-1998. Sadly she died in office.

As with most Internet stories, Shanda, dog mayor, is noted in a single paragraph that cycles from site to site with a few changes. This is a somewhat old story so thought I ought to touch bases with the people involved so that I had some new information to share. To begin with, I could not locate Shanda's owner who no longer seems to live near Guffey. I believe I found him in Florida but he did not return my call so I turned to the people of Guffey.

Guffey is a small mountain town and has its own website on which I found a telephone number that seemed to be for tourism-type calls. My call to that number was answered promptly by Charlie Morreale, who identified himself as an employee at Guffey's Garage. (The website mentions that Guffey's Garage is no longer a working auto garage; the site says "we can help you with propane, ice, and custom welding jobs. We also carry an assortment of new and used plumbing and electrical supplies.") The Garage people also seem to have collected "oddities." If you want to see the museum's collection, "ask for the key at the Garage" and you can let yourself in. Love it...just like a New York museum!

But back to Shanda, the Dog Mayor. I asked Charlie about Shanda, and his reply was a guffaw: "Boy are you out of touch!"

"I know that Shanda's term ended in 1998," I replied. "I'm calling to find out who replaced Shanda." I had learned from the previous information that Shanda was unique in being a canine mayor. The "Democats" had dominated since 1988 when a cat named Paisley was elected mayor. Paisley died and was replaced by Smudge le Plume. Sadly Smudge was murdered by an unapprehended owl, and a third cat, Whiffey le Gone, was then elected.

Whiffey was forced to step down when her owners moved to a ranch. This left an opening for Shanda, whose owner was quoted as stating that Shanda was against any leash law, and "unlike other politicians, she really does listen to you."

About the Current Mayor

After Shanda died in office, "Monster the Cat" became mayor and is now serving a second term. (Monster is owned by Bill Soux who also owns the Guffey Garage.)

Charlie added that schoolchildren are the voters for the mayoral election. (Thank you, Charlie, I would have assumed it was the townspeople and would not have thought to ask if there was a different electorate.)

Charlie also noted that Guffey's population is about 20 people and that Guffey has a fire department, a public works office, a library, a community center, two bars, and three restaurants. When I asked Charlie to explain the animals' mayoral responsibilities, he said, "You're serious aren't you?" He then continued: "Well, Monster shows up here every morning for breakfast and then he goes out and spends the day politickin'."

As nearly as I can tell from the website, Guffey relies on tourism to a great degree so the idea of having a cat or a dog as mayor is actually brilliant, but I was concerned about the fact that there were still issues like firefighting and trash removal that needed to be taken care of. I made several more phone calls and learned that Guffey is unincorporated and is part of Park County. Tom Locke at *The Flume*, a website that covers news from Guffey, informed me there are at least two local boards: a school board and a fire department board of directors. The Park County Sheriff's Office provides law enforcement services, and trash removal is carried out by a private company, probably as part of a county contract. (I did not get responses from a good number of the people I contacted, but my timing was bad. Fairplay, a nearby community, was having their annual Burro Pack Race that weekend.)

From the people I reached, it seems that Guffey's services are well taken care of, and therefore, a mayoral figurehead that attracts publicity is probably a very wise move.

More about the Mayor

While searching for a little more information about the sitting mayor, I came upon Monster's MySpace page. The page gives Monster's age as 22. (I hope the community is grooming a successor.) It notes that Monster serves "with disinterest and occasional violent outbursts against tourists and local animals."

Under music preferences, Monster specifies "No violins!" and notes that television "rots your brain, but I do like Judge Judy."

As to whom Monster would like to meet: "Other independent elected officials. Preferably pussies. Dick Cheney." (Not clear whether Cheney is on a separate list or considered part of the former grouping.)

Monster's hero? "The guy with the sardines."

Book preferences? "I can't read, [expletive]. I'm a cat. And don't get smart about how I created this page. I'm dictating."

We will now return to stories about dogs. But Shanda and Monster and Guffey were too good to pass up.

Now we will take a look at some First Dogs.

PART TWO:

DOGS THAT LIVED
AT THE WHITE HOUSE

FIRST DOG, BO OBAMA

Campaign promises are important, and none more so than a campaign promise made by a candidate to his family.

Few dog lovers will forget the words spoken on Election Night 2008 by President-Elect Barack Obama: "Sasha and Malia, I love you both more than you can imagine. You have earned the puppy that is coming with us."

Throughout the campaign of 2008, Obama had indicated that win or lose, the one thing he could guarantee was that his girls would get a puppy after the election.

Though the Obamas had hoped to adopt a dog from a shelter, Malia's allergies placed priority on getting a hypoallergenic breed. This led them to Portuguese Water Dogs. (While doctors dispute the reality of "hypoallergenic," breeds like the PWD don't shed, so the likelihood of stirring up allergies is reduced.)

Portuguese Water Dogs were a breed favored by Senator Ted Kennedy, who was still alive at the outset of Obama's term. As the family needs became known, Kennedy wanted to give the Obama children a dog from his breeder, Julie Parker. Bo, then called Charlie, was born to Penny (from the Amigo Kennel); his father was Watson (Valkyrie Kennel).

Bo had actually been placed with another family where it had not worked out, so he had been returned to the breeder as is the custom with pure-bred dogs. Kennedy arranged for his own obedience trainer to work with Bo to assure that he would be welcome at the White House.

Bo officially arrived at 1600 Pennsylvania Avenue on April 14, 2009. His tuxedo coloring–black coat, white chest, and white front paws–made him an instant favorite with photographers, and the family clearly was thrilled with the joyful and energetic pup.

Bo's full name is Amigo's New Hope, but Malia and Sasha decided to call him Bo. Their cousins have a cat named Bo, and Michelle Obama's father was nicknamed Diddley (as in Bo Diddley).

About the Breed

The Portuguese Water Dog is classified by the American Kennel Club as a working dog. They are fine and enthusiastic swimmers, and many years ago, fishermen in the Algarve region of Portugal discovered the dogs could be taught to herd fish into nets, to retrieve lost tackle and broken nets, and to act as couriers from ship to ship, or ship to shore.

While Bo keeps a low profile at the White House, he is occasionally seen by visitors. When Michelle Obama meets with schoolchildren, she is frequently asked about Bo, and from her descriptions, Bo sounds like a very normal and much-loved canine family member.

And as it happened, Bo stole the show when the First Lady paid a visit to young patients at the Children's National Medical Center during the 2012 holidays. She was there to read the children the holiday classic "Twas the Night Before Christmas."

Bo went along and after checking out the beautifully decorated tree behind the First Lady, Bo jumped into Mrs. Obama's lap, where he remained, legs dangling, as she read the entire story.

"This is exactly what he does at home," Mrs. Obama was quoted as saying. "He tries to beat Malia and Sasha to my lap."

KATE KELLY

THE BUSH FAMILIES AND THEIR DOGS

There is no doubt that the Bush family members who lived in the White House are "dog people." The photos of the two families depict people who absolutely relish being with their animals.

George H.W. Bush (41) and his wife Barbara lived in the White House from 1989-1993 and brought with them their Springer spaniel, Millie. Millie had at least one litter of puppies. One of the puppies, Ranger, stayed at the White House with George and Barbara.

Another puppy, Spot, was given to George W. and Laura who eventually brought Spot back to the White House when they moved in. (This was the first time the country had a second-generation First Dog).

In addition to giving birth to a future First Dog, Millie also wrote a book. Barbara Bush thought Millie would be the perfect voice to tell the behind-the-scenes story of the White House. Millie describes a day in the life of George Herbert Walker Bush and family, discussing morning briefings, deliberations in the Oval Office, and of course, her own short breaks for squirrel hunting. Both children and adults enjoyed the book, and it remained on the bestseller list for many weeks. For Barbara Bush, the book was important because it gave her an additional way to raise money for literacy.

George and Laura

When George W. Bush (43) and wife Laura moved into the White House in 2001, they brought with them Millie's offspring, Spot, then age 11, and Barney, a young Scotty. The dogs ingratiated themselves with most people at the White House, however, in 2008, Barney did take issue with a Reuters reporter who tried to pet him. This was the only known Barney biting incident, so after the initial flurry of headlines—and some antibiotics for the reporter—life for the dogs at the White House returned to normal.

Total joy is reflected in almost all photos of George and Laura Bush and the dogs. However, in scanning through the photos, there are a few of Barney that will give any dog owner a laugh: Barney had no interest in boarding the presidential helicopter. Reports were that if he were to accompany the first family, he had to be followed, nabbed, and carried on to the chopper.

On January 6, 2005, after Spot's death, President Bush gave Laura a new Scottish terrier for her birthday. Miss Beazley started her time at the White House as you might expect—with a press conference.

Barney was never in danger of being eclipsed by the newcomer. During the Bush White House years, Barney had his own website, and each year at the holiday, the family would release videos of a Barney-eye view of life at the White House. These videos are no longer available on a government website but they can be found on YouTube.

THE DOGS OF RONALD REAGAN

Ronald and Nancy Reagan were definitely "animal people." Before, during, and after the presidency (spanning from 1981-89), Ronald Reagan was frequently seen on horseback, often accompanied by Nancy. In 1987, the press was nearby when he was in Nebraska about to go off on a ride and he left them with this comment: "I've often said that there is nothing better for the inside of a man than the outside of a horse."

A family dog offers a more convenient way to enjoy animals, and the Reagans always had them though they did not initially bring any of their own dogs to Washington. The first dog to join them at the White House was a tiny ball of black fluff that was presented to them in 1985 by the young girl who was serving as the poster girl for the March of Dimes. The dog was named Lucky, and that tiny ball of fluff was actually a Bouvier des Flandres that quickly grew to "be the size of a pony," according to Nancy. Lucky was frequently seen thundering down the halls in the West Wing of the White House.

Nancy later noted that Lucky's favorite moments were at Camp David where he had room to run. He knew that if he were being loaded onto the helicopter, then the odds were good that he was going to Camp David, and his excitement knew no bounds. His favorite seat on the copter? Preferably the President's lap.

The Reagans soon decided that living at the White House was not right for Lucky, so they sent him to live at the Reagan ranch where there was plenty of space to run as well as other dogs to play with, including Victory, a golden retriever, and Scotch and Soda, black Scottish terriers.

Rex

The White House was not dog-less for long. On December 6, 1985 Ronald Reagan gave Nancy a Cavalier King Charles Spaniel for Christmas. One of Rex's first jobs was helping to throw the switch to light the White House Christmas tree.

The Lincoln bedroom has long been rumored to be haunted, and Rex agreed. According to a Washington correspondent for the *Glasgow Herald* (4/23/88), Rex took a strong dislike to the room and wouldn't enter. He stood at the doorway, looked in, and barked.

Rex's dog house was grander than any the White House dogs had owned previously. Designed by Theo Hayes, great-great-grandson of President Rutherford Hayes, who also had dogs at the White House, the dog house was white clapboard with red velvet drapes and framed photos of the President and First Lady that hung on the interior walls.

When Rex and the Reagans moved out of the White House at the end of Reagan's second term, Rex must have planned to leave his elegant dog house for the next four-legged resident, as he was presented with a new dog house that was a replica of the White House. Lining the inside was a patch of carpet from Camp David.

Ron and Nancy took their pets very seriously, and when an animal died, the president personally buried them in a little hilltop cemetery created especially for the Reagan pets on their ranch near Santa Barbara. It was said that he also carved a headstone for each animal that died so they always would be remembered.

Also a First Fish

Early in the presidency, Ronald Reagan was shot by John Hinckley, Jr. in an assassination attempt. Americans were quite concerned about the president, and one ten-year-old boy sent the president the best gift he could think of—a goldfish enclosed in a water-filled plastic bag. The Reagans accepted the gift with graciousness and the goldfish spent the remainder of its life with Ron and Nancy.

This type of thing was business as usual for the Reagans, and the fish story would not have surprised daughter Patti Davis, who was estranged from her parents up until shortly before Reagan's death in 2004. At Ronald Reagan's funeral, Ms. Davis recalled how her father gave a funeral to her own pet goldfish when she was growing up (*New York Times*, 6-12-2004).

"We went out into the garden and we dug a tiny grave with a teaspoon," she said. "And he took two twigs and lashed them together with twine and formed a cross as a marker for the grave. And then he gave a beautiful eulogy. He told me that my fish was swimming in the clear blue waters in heaven. And he would never tire and he would never get hungry and he would never be in any danger. And he could swim as far and wide as he wanted. And he never had to stop because the river went on forever. He was free."

KATE KELLY

GERALD AND BETTY FORD'S
GOLDEN RETRIEVER, LIBERTY

Betty and Gerald Ford had owned two golden retrievers before they moved into the White House, but sadly their most recent dog died before Ford assumed the presidency. Daughter Susan entered into a conspiracy with White House photographer David Hume Kennerly to remedy the Ford family's "dogless" state. Kennerly agreed to call around to breeders who might have pups available; both he and Susan felt anonymity in calling was important. Kennerly soon located an 8-month-old dog from a good breeder in Minnesota.

When David and Susan followed up, the breeder was cautious. He wanted to be certain that his dog would be well-placed, and the screening began. He asked who the dog's owner would be, and David and Susan said they were not able to say. The kennel owner said they couldn't have one of his pups then because he didn't do business that way; he needed to know the dog was going to a good home.

David and Susan assured him the dog would be in a good home–that it would live with a couple and their four children and they had owned golden retrievers before.

"What kind of a house do they live in?" And here the stories diverge. David and Susan reported that they said, "a big white house with a fence around it." But Ford wrote in his memoir, that there was a question about whether the family owned or rented, and David replied: "I guess you might call it public housing."

The questions continued: Did the father have a steady job so buying enough food for a big dog wouldn't be an issue? Given that the presidency is not a steady job, David and Susan agreed at that point that they were never going to get the dog without specifying that the dog was to live at 1600 Pennsylvania Avenue.

They revealed the truth, and a deal was made. Susan brought the dog, originally named Streaker, to the White House where she surprised her father by letting Liberty (the name Susan chose for her) introduce herself with a run around the Oval Office. In his memoir, Ford writes of his delight at the four-legged surprise and remembered immediately getting down on the floor to play with the dog.

Memorable Remarks from Ford

On October 9, 1974 Ford gave a speech in Philadelphia where he was honoring William Scranton. (Ford later appointed Scranton to be U.S. Ambassador to the United Nations.)

In an aside, he told the following story: "A reporter happened to ask Susan who is going to take care of Liberty; who is going to feed her and groom her and take her out each night or every morning? Susan did not hesitate one minute. She said, 'Of course, it will be Dad,' So I have this feeling–this is one Liberty that is going to cost me some of mine."

President Ford concluded with this additional thought: "But in a broader sense, that is the true nature of liberty. It comes with both privileges and obligations. Freedom, we all know, is seldom free."

KATE KELLY

KATE KELLY

LBJ'S DOGS, HIM AND HER

Him and Her, two beagles born in June of 1963 were certainly the best-known pets of Lyndon Baines Johnson, 36th president of the United States (1963-69). The Johnsons were frequently photographed with the dogs. One notable photograph shows the President "howling" with one of the beagles. Another famous photograph made a big stir for the White House.

President Johnson was taking a break outside at the White House with a task force of 13 gentlemen who were meeting to discuss ways to encourage more foreign investment in the United States. The dogs were walking along with the group when the President decided to encourage Him to bark; he lifted the dog to his haunches by pulling up on his ears.

No one with the group that day seemed to think much about the occurrence, but the moment was captured by a photographer. The photograph of the "ear lift" was published in *Life* magazine. The reaction from the public was immediate, and the White House was flooded with telegrams, phone calls, and letters.

Experts weighed in. An official at the American Society for the Prevention of Cruelty to Animals was quoted as saying, "If someone picked you up by the ears, you'd yelp, too." And beagle experts noted that it was indeed common practice in hunt country "to tug the dogs' ears to be sure they are in good voice."

But Lyndon Johnson soon found that the only way out of the mess was to say he was sorry. He apologized publicly but later told reporters in an aside that "he had been pulling Him's ears since he was a pup, and he seemed to like it."

Him was bred with another beagle in 1965, and two of that litter, Freckles and Kim, were given to Luci Johnson to keep as pets. After her marriage to Patrick Nugent and subsequent move out of the White House, one beagle, Kim, went to live with the Nugents but Freckles remained at the White House.

Both Him and Her died at young ages. Her swallowed a stone in 1964 and died from it; Him was hit by a car in 1966 when he was chasing a squirrel across the White House property.

Other Dogs during the LBJ Years

After Him died, J. Edgar Hoover, director of the Federal Bureau of Investigation, presented Johnson with another beagle. The President named the dog J. Edgar but soon shortened it to Edgar. When Johnson left the White House, Edgar accompanied the Johnson's to the LBJ Ranch.

Blanco was another dog who lived with the Johnsons at the White House. He was a white collie given to the president in December of 1963 as a gift from a little girl in Illinois. Before moving back to Texas, the Johnsons gave Blanco to a doctor and his wife in Kentucky.

Yuki was a mutt found by Luci Nugent at a gas station in Texas in 1966. Yuki (the name means snow) was adopted by Luci, but after LBJ met Yuki, it became clear that they were meant for each other. Luci presented Yuki to her father for his birthday in 1967. Yuki remained with the Johnsons until after Lyndon's death in 1973; Yuki spent her final years with Luci and her family.

KATE KELLY

EISENHOWER'S WEIMERANER, HEIDI

During their time in the White House (1953-1961), Ike and Mamie Eisenhower simplified their lives by keeping animals to a minimum. They had only two pets during this time, a never-photographed parakeet and a rarely photographed Weimeraner named Heidi.

In the 1950s when Heidi lived at the White House, the Weimeraner was still a relatively unusual dog to be owned by a family in the United States. Originally these dogs were bred by Germans as hunting dogs. However, the Weimeraner was unique because unlike most hunting dogs that usually lived in a kennel with other dogs, the Weimeraner was an all-purpose family dog. It could be taken hunting but was also very loyal to the family, serving both as guard dog of the home and playmate to the family's children.

Up until the late 1800s, any Weimeraner sold for use in America was sterilized as the Germans did not want Americans to popularize the breed and change its basic attributes, which included great hunting skills as well as a lively and pleasant disposition.

By the early 1900s, this practice had changed and dogs were being sold more freely. However, most Americans in the 1950s were more likely to own mutts than a pure breed dog; a dog like Heidi would still have been an uncommon sight. (Today the Weimeraner is probably best known for being the breed of dog owned by artist William Wegman, who has captured the dogs in still photography, posing as Little Red Riding Hood and countless other characters, as well as making appearances on shows like Sesame Street.)

On its website, the Eisenhower library quotes a letter from Eisenhower in 1958 to Arthur Summerfield (1899-1972) from whom the Eisenhowers had received the dog: "Heidi is definitely an asset to life in the White House. She cavorts on the South Lawn at a great rate, with such important projects as chasing squirrels and investigating what might be under bushes. She is beautiful and well-behaved (occasionally she tends toward stubbornness but is then immediately apologetic about it). And she is extremely affectionate and seemingly happy. I am constantly indebted to you for giving her to me."

In addition to providing the Eisenhowers with Heidi, Arthur Summerfield served as postmaster general for Eisenhower from 1953-61.

However, any dog owner will identify with the Eisenhowers' likely chagrin when Heidi left a good-sized yellow stain on the carpet in the Diplomatic Reception Room in the White House. However, unlike most of us, Mamie and Ike were probably not expected to clean it up.

Though Heidi was mostly unseen around 1600 Pennsylvania Avenue, I received a note from one reader who remembered Heidi. The reader was a child in Washington, D.C. while Eisenhower was in office. She and her father had been out for a stroll, and they had purchased ice cream cones. As they walked along the fence near the White House, Heidi appeared. The reader could not resist offering Heidi a lick of her ice cream cone. A great memory to have!

By 1961 Heidi had made the out-of-office transition to the Eisenhowers' farm in Gettysburg, where she gave birth to at least one litter of puppies.

KATE KELLY

FALA, FDR'S BELOVED DOG

The year was 1940 and Franklin Delano Roosevelt (1882-1945), the 32nd president of the United States had been in office since 1933, governing through the years of the Great Depression and attempting to maintain U.S. neutrality despite the onset of fighting in Europe.

That November President Roosevelt's cousin, Margaret Suckley, brought him a six-month old Scottish terrier, a gift from Miss Katherine Davies of Westport, Connecticut. The puppy lightened the President's spirits and captivated his heart.

FDR embraced having Fala around at all times, and Fala–usually looked after by Margaret Suckley–traveled with FDR, slept on a special chair at the end of the president's bed, and was generally hand-fed his dinner by FDR. Dignitaries often waited for President Roosevelt to join them for dinner; Roosevelt himself like to feed Fala, and this "very important dinner" took place before any others were served.

Life at the White House

In 1943 a 13-year-old girl from Massachusetts wrote to the president inquiring about the origin of Fala's name. On behalf of the president, a secretary replied: "…his kennel name Fala was after a remote ancestor of the President whose name was Murray, the outlaw of Fala Hill. Fala Hill was his ancestral estate in Scotland and he was descended through many generations of Murrays." (*The New York Times*, 12-24-43)

The Secret Service referred to Fala as "The Informer." Because Fala had to be taken outside for walks, anyone who saw Fala on one of his outdoor visits would have known the president was nearby.

While there is no doubt how much FDR loved Fala, Fala also was used to facilitate communication with the public. When the U.S. was encouraging everyone to make sacrifices as part of the war effort, Fala did, too. The White House released a photo of Fala with the rubber toys he had committed to donating to a rubber collection drive. The government encouraged other dog owners to follow Fala's lead.

Letters to Fala were written, often by the owner in the voice of his or her dog. One offered to share her flower bed full of bones with Fala; another wanted to know what Fala ate. A secretary wrote back: "…it is too difficult to describe, but consists of various diets of all kinds which are prescribed by a veterinary." (Fala's files are kept at Hyde Park, along with the rest of the presidential papers.)

In 1943 MGM requested permission to make a movie of Fala's life in the White House (supporting cast included the president and Diane Hopkins, the young daughter of Harry Hopkins; Hopkins was one of Roosevelt's closest advisors). Theodore Strauss of The New York Times writes on April 25, 1943 of the film crew's experience: The crew must have missed shots of Fala chasing the White House squirrels, so they borrowed a squirrel from the zoo, and when they released this "new" squirrel from the cage, Fala gleefully chased it, just as he did the native White House squirrels. Fala also avidly read the scrapbook of his news clippings–after the crew hid bits of bacon around the pages.

Fala and the Election

In 1944, the country was preoccupied with the war. Before the presidential campaign was fully underway, GOP operatives accused FDR of leaving Fala in the Aleutian Islands and then sending a destroyer back to find him, with taxpayers bearing the cost of the trip. The Navy denied this report, so Minnesota Representative Harold Knutson (R) demanded that the House of Representatives look into whether government money was spent to go back to the Islands to retrieve Fala. (Honestly, with all of Fala's handlers, the odds of him having been left behind seem very remote.)

Roosevelt opened his re-election campaign with a speech to the Teamsters Union in Washington, D.C., on September 23, 1944, and after covering several important issues, Roosevelt won over the room with comments about Fala:

"These Republican leaders have not been content with attacks on me, or my wife, or on my sons. No, not content with that, they now include my little dog, Fala. Well, of course, I don't resent attacks, and my family doesn't resent attacks, but Fala does resent them. You know, Fala is Scotch, and being a Scottie, as soon as he learned that the Republican fiction writers in Congress and out[side Congress] had concocted a story that I had left him behind on the Aleutian Islands and had sent a destroyer back to find him—at a cost to the taxpayers of two or three, or eight or twenty million dollars—his Scotch soul was furious. He has not been the same dog since. I am accustomed to hearing malicious falsehoods about myself—such as that old, worm-eaten chestnut that I have represented myself as indispensable. But I think I have a right to resent, to object to libelous statements about my dog."

The room filled with Teamsters loved it. And they loved him.

Fala outlived the President by seven years. The little dog spent the remainder of his life with Eleanor, living with her at her apartment across from Washington Square in Greenwich Village or staying with her at her house, Val-Kill, near Hyde Park.

In her autobiography Eleanor wrote poignantly of an occasion when General Eisenhower visited the Roosevelt estate to lay a wreath on the president's grave: "When Fala heard the sirens [of the police escort accompanying Eisenhower], his legs straightened out, his ears pricked up, and I knew that he expected to see his master coming down the drive…"

Fala died in 1952 and is buried at Hyde Park next to Franklin and Eleanor.

THE DOGS OF HERBERT HOOVER

The 31st president of the United States, Herbert Hoover (1874-1964) and his wife, Lou, both loved dogs. As it happens, a dog helped Herbert Hoover get elected in 1928.

The dog in question, a German shepherd named King Tut, was acquired by Hoover when Hoover was in Belgium on assignment for President Wilson. Hoover was running a war relief organization for Europe after World War I. While overseas, Hoover adopted his "police dog," as they were commonly known, and after his assignment was completed, Hoover brought King Tut back to America.

With a stellar record for his service as a wartime food administrator. Hoover was a logical pick to be the presidential candidate in 1928. However even then political handlers existed. They knew that in order for the very serious and very private Herbert Hoover to be elected, he needed to be presented to the public in a lovable and relatable way.

The solution? Play up Hoover's natural affection for King Tut. A photograph was taken of a smiling Hoover with King Tut's paws in Hoover's hands as if the dog were also vote-begging. Adorned with Hoover's signature, the photo was mailed out to voters across the United States. It worked.

Other Dogs in the White House

While King Tut was Hoover's favorite, the White House was filled with dogs during the Hoovers' time there. There were two fox terriers named Big Ben and Sonnie, a Scotch collie named Glen, a Malamut called Yukon, a setter named Eaglehurst Gillette, another German shepherd, Pat, and Weejie, the elkhound.

Once they were in the White House, Lou Hoover received an uncommon dog as a gift. A classmate of Lou's raised Irish wolfhounds—a very unusual breed for America at the time—and the breeder presented to Lou a dog whose pedigree name was Cragwood Padraic, called Patrick by the Hoovers.

The White House did not bring happiness to the Hoovers or to King Tut. King Tut took as his responsibility full-time guarding of the president. In addition to patrolling the perimeter of 1600 Pennsylvania Avenue, King Tut was watchful over all visitors to the White House, and the strain proved to be too much for him. He quit eating, so Hoover sent him to a quiet home, hoping he would recover. Unfortunately, Tut's health failed to improve, and he died. (Veterinarians today would likely have a different diagnosis.)

By this time the stock market had crashed and Hoover did not release the news about Tut, knowing that with the pain of the economic devastation people were facing, news about a dog having died would not be helpful to the perception of the first family.

In 1932, Hoover ran again for president, without Tut, but was resoundingly defeated by Franklin D. Roosevelt, who brought other dogs—and eventually better news—to the White House.

KATE KELLY

THE COOLIDGE DOGS
(AND OTHER ANIMALS)

If the American population divided itself into pet people and non-pet people, Calvin Coolidge–our 30th president (1923-1929)–and his wife Grace, would definitely be on the "pet" side of the line. They had cats, birds, two pet raccoons, and of course, dogs.

Peter Pan, a terrier, came with the Coolidges to the White House but he did not like the hustle and bustle of Washington life, so the Coolidges found a quieter home for him. Paul Pry, an Airedale, was the next dog to arrive, and he was fiercely loyal to the Coolidges, to the point that he wouldn't permit the housekeepers to enter a room where the president was.

Rob Roy and Prudence Prim were two white collies that joined the family. Prudence was a particular favorite of Grace's.

Beans was a Boston bulldog who arrived and took position as lead dog, which put Rob's nose out of joint so the Coolidges gave Beans to Mrs. Coolidge's mother who lived in Northampton, Massachusetts.

Tiny Tim and Blackberry were chows. Tiny Tim soon became "Terrible Tim" in the president's eyes, so he was soon moved to other quarters. The family picked up Blackberry on a trip to the Black Hills. Blackberry was all black including the inside of her mouth, and she became a gift to their son John Coolidge's "intended."

Calamity Jane was a Shetland sheepdog who joined the family, but there were still more dogs to come (though not all were at the White House). There were two other collies, Bessie and Ruby Rouch, and a German shepherd named King Cole. There was also a bird dog named Palo Alto.

A Raccoon Named Rebecca
and Ducks in the Bathroom

The Coolidges also created homes for many other animals. Rebecca was a live raccoon given to the Coolidges to be served as part of Thanksgiving dinner, but Grace Coolidge wouldn't hear of it! She had a pen built encircling a tree on the White House grounds. They acquired a friend for her, Reuben, but he soon escaped. Rebecca, however, seemed happy with her White House digs and her regular meals.

Over the years of the presidency, the Coolidges received a wallaby, a bobcat, a black bear, a donkey, a Pygmy hippo, and two lion cubs (named Tax Reduction and Budget

Bureau), a duiker (a small antelope), and 13 Pekin ducks (a type of domestic duck from Long Island). The Coolidges attempted to raise the ducks in one of the bathrooms in the White House, but they soon became too large, and along with the other more exotic animals, had to be given to the zoo.

KATE KELLY

LADDIE BOY,
WARREN HARDING'S DOG

Laddie Boy was an Airedale belonging to Warren G. Harding, the 29th president of the United States (1921-23). Had Harding lived to serve a longer term of office, Laddie Boy might be as well remembered as Fala or LBJ's beagles.

No dog before or after Harding received as much press coverage as did Laddie Boy. Harding started his career as a newspaper man, eventually becoming full owner of the *Marion Daily Star* in Ohio. Perhaps for that reason, he was willing to provide access to Laddie Boy that most presidents do not give.

Born on July 26, 1920 at the Caswell Kennels in Toledo, Ohio, Laddie Boy was six months old when he arrived at the White House on March 5, 1921, the day after Harding's inauguration. Harding had asked that he be told as soon as the dog arrived, and indeed, a cabinet meeting was interrupted so that Harding could see his new pup.

Seven days later, a reporter for the *New York Times* wrote of Laddie Boy's having learned to carry the paper to the breakfast table to deliver it to the President. "The Airedale has been working on the 'stunt' for several days but this was the first time he got through it without a hitch..." (3-12-1921)

Laddie Boy's Birthday

While the White House has kennels for owners who want to keep their dogs there, the Hardings kept Laddie Boy with them at almost all times. He participated in the logical "photo op" events such as the Easter Egg roll on the White House lawn, but he also had his own chair to sit in during cabinet meetings.

On Laddie Boy's first birthday at the White House, the press corps was given photo access to snap pictures of the First Dog with a dog-biscuit birthday cake sent him from Ohio by his father Champion Tintern Tip Top. His father had also supposedly penned an encouraging letter to his famous son "whose pictures appear so often in the newspapers and magazines..." Along with the cake, the kennel enclosed some invitations for Laddie Boy to send out to his favorite canines or humans so that they could be invited to attend his party (7-24-1922).

Harding also wrote to the press in Laddie's voice expressing Laddie Boy's opinions on things. In one letter, Laddie Boy wrote of life in the White House: "So many people express a wish to see me, and I shake hands with so many callers at the Executive Mansion that I fear there are some people who will suspect me of political inclinations.

From what I see of politics, I am sure I have no such aspirations." (*New York Times*, 2-8-1922)

In July of 1923 the Hardings wanted to escape Washington where the press corps was working overtime looking into the scandals that arose during Harding's presidency (among them the Teapot Dome scandal). President Harding and the First Lady planned a trip to visit the West Coast and Alaska (Harding was the first president to visit Alaska).

President Harding was feeling the stress, and over the course of a few weeks, his bouts of "not feeling well' became worse, and on August 2, 1923, Harding passed away in San Francisco. Laddie Boy had not accompanied them on the trip, and newspaper reporters made note of the fact that there was no way to explain Harding's absence to one White House member, Laddie Boy.

Harding's reputation as a "newspaper man" was well known, and Louis Newman, President of the Roosevelt Newsboys' Association hit upon a way to create a unique tribute to President Harding. He asked newsboys across the nation to donate one penny a piece in memory of the president. The plan was to take the pennies and melt them down so that they could be sculpted into a statue of Laddie Boy. Nineteen thousand one hundred thirty-four pennies were collected from boys all over the nation. Laddie Boy sat patiently for some 15 sittings so a sculptor could capture his image. The sculpture was completed and now belongs to the Smithsonian Institution (copies are rare but can sometimes be found on eBay).

Shortly after the president's death, Mrs. Harding wanted to reward Secret Service agent Harry L. Barker for his kindness to the couple, so she suggested that Barker should have Laddie Boy. Barker was soon transferred to the Boston office, and Laddie Boy lived out the rest of his life with the

Barkers in Boston. The newspapers took note of the dog's death from 'old age' in 1930. Florence Harding died of renal failure in 1924 so it was fortunate that Laddie Boy had already been placed in a loving home.

TEDDY ROOSEVELT'S DOGS

When Vice President Teddy Roosevelt assumed the presidency after William McKinley died of a gunshot wound sustained in Buffalo, New York in 1901, life at the White House underwent quite a change. McKinley and his wife, Ida, had lived quietly at 1600 Pennsylvania Avenue with their parrot and a cat. They were childless, having lost two daughters when the children were young.

When Teddy and Edith Roosevelt arrived in Washington with six children and a host of animals, the residence was anything but quiet. They filled the White House with life and laughter. The Roosevelts were in the White House from 1901-1909.

Many Dogs

The Roosevelt dogs included Rollo, a friendly St. Bernard, Sailor Boy, a Chesapeake retriever, and Manchu, a black Pekingese given to daughter Alice by the last empress of China.

Blackjack was a Manchester terrier who had the misfortune of being terrified of the family cat, Tom Quartz. The cat tormented Jack by chasing him away whenever the dog came near.

Pete, a bull terrier, was finally exiled from the White House for having nipped too many visitors' ankles. The dog used up his last chance when he ripped the pants of the French ambassador. Pete was sent to live at Sagamore Hill, the family home on Long Island.

Edith Roosevelt favored mixed breeds, and the first lady had a mongrel named Tip, followed by one named Mutt.

Other Pets

The Roosevelt family also had many other pets. At one point there was a small bear named Jonathan Edwards, a lizard named Bill, a macaw named Eli Yale, a pig named Maude, snakes, a one-legged rooster, and a pony named Algonquin.

When son Archie was sick, his brothers wanted to cheer him up so they helped the pony get into the White House elevator and took Algonquin up to Archie's room. The children were delighted. The adults, with the exception of TR, were likely less so.

TR's Favorite

The president's favorite dog was Skip, a small mutt (possibly a rat terrier) that Roosevelt found when he was on a bear hunt in the Grand Canyon. Roosevelt reported that Skip could stand his ground against anything–something Roosevelt felt he often had to do himself when facing Congress.

Skip was also a popular playmate of Archie's. When Archie was 7, he invented a game that involved racing Skip down the polished hallways of the White House. As Roosevelt described it, Archie would place Skip between his legs and bend over holding on to the dog. Then he would count, "On your mark, Skip, Ready! Go!"

And Archie gave Skip a bit of a backward shove as he propelled himself forward to run quickly down the hall. Skip would skitter on the smooth hardwood floors trying to get his footing to chase after Archie. Skip lost every time but it didn't seem to dampen his enthusiasm to play the game again and again.

When the children had gone to bed, Skip had one more task. Roosevelt often read after dinner, so Skip would find the president and hop onto his lap for a nap.

Roosevelt was known to have said that perhaps no family enjoyed the White House more than they did. He's probably right.

THE ANIMALS OF RUTHERFORD B. HAYES

Rutherford B. Hayes (1822-1893) served the country honorably and held to the reforms he believed in, yet he is best remembered as "Rutherfraud B. Hayes" or "Old 8 to 7" for the manner in which he won the election of 1876.

Both Hayes, a Republican, and the Democratic candidate Samuel Tilden were in favor of certain reforms–hard money (a return to the gold standard) and a way to give out civil service jobs that did not involve patronage. Tilden was the better known, but the Republicans campaigned hard. The result was a popular vote win for Tilden but there was no electoral college winner, and twenty electoral votes were in dispute. (Tilden only needed one of the electoral votes for a win, but Hayes needed all twenty.)

To devise a path forward, Congress established an electoral commission, and despite basic intentions to arrange for a neutral commission, the Republicans held sway. When the commission ruled in favor of Hayes, the Democrats intended to filibuster to prevent Congress from accepting the votes. A back room deal was struck. Hayes was deemed winner of the election, and he agreed to accept the end of federal occupation of the South as well as a government subsidy for a Southern rail line. This was known as the Compromise of 1877.

On to the White House

Rutherford B. Hayes and his wife, Lucy, moved into the White House with their children and many animals. Lucy (known as "Lemonade Lucy" for her refusal to serve alcohol at the White House) was said to love animals–and they her, so pets were very much a part of the Hayes household. (Given the level of photographic development of the time there are no images of the Hayes' dogs.)

The Hayes' had several dogs: Jet, a mutt; Deke, an English mastiff; Hector, a Newfoundland; Dot, a cocker spaniel; two shepherd dogs, Hector and Nellie, and two hunting dogs. (It is not clear exactly which dogs were with them in Washington.) A two-year-old greyhound named Grim was given to Mrs. Hayes by Mrs. William DuPont of Wilmington, Delaware. In the President's diary, he notes that the dog "took all our hearts at once."

In research provided by Nan Card, the manuscripts curator at the Hayes Presidential Center, she writes that "One day, as Lucy sang the 'Star Spangled Banner,' Grim lifted up his head and howled in a most pitiful manner. And ever after, when his mistress sang the national anthem, Grim began to howl.

"But if Hayes and the children were exceedingly fond of their 'large, handsome' greyhound, it was Lucy whom Grim loved best. Hayes recalled, 'How happy old Grim always was when she returned after an absence'."

Grim accompanied the family in their move to Spiegel Grove, Ohio, and there Grim was joined by two of his own pups: Juno and Jove.

The curator's report continues: "Wagons and carriages turned aside for him [Grim] wherever he went. But Grim's privileged status may have been his undoing. One spring day, while running on the Lake Shore Railroad tracks, Grim encountered an oncoming train. Instead of moving aside, he 'stopped still.' The engineer blew his whistle repeatedly, but Grim 'did not stir.' Death was instantaneous. The president could only conclude that Grim fully expected 'the train to turn out for him.'"

Other Animals at the White House

Given the time period, the Hayes White House also kept several carriage horses, Jersey cows and a goat (probably for milking) as well as four canaries and a mockingbird.

Rutherford and Lucy also received several kittens, and one of them, Siam, was said to be the first Siamese cat brought to America. Siam was a gift from David B. Sickels, a U.S. diplomat posted in Bangkok. Siam was a favorite of Hayes' daughter Fanny. When Siam became ill, the president's own physician was summoned to provide care for the cat. Unfortunately Siam did not recover, and instructions were given to preserve her body, however, according to the Hayes Presidential Center, a stuffed version of Siam has never been found.

Though he had hoped to make further progress on civil service reform and abolish the color line in the country, he served as well as he could, given the atmosphere. However, he remained true to his intention to serve only one term.

When he retired he devoted his time to education reform and working with other activists to find viable answers to what was referred to as the Negro Question. He died of a heart attack in 1893.

Rutherford Hayes is the first president to have a presidential library–something that is now a tradition. The Hayes Presidential Center is located in Spiegel Grove, Ohio where the family once lived with their children and animals.

GEORGE WASHINGTON'S POODLE
AND OTHER DOGS

George Washington was said to have been a man who loved dogs and owned many. He was an avid hunter, and most of his dogs would have been used for hunting.

The Marquis de Lafayette was known to have sent seven staghounds to George Washington in a sign of friendship. A photo of this breed shows a likeness to what we know today as greyhounds. In colonial times, these dogs were great hunters, but they were bred to hunt via speed and sight; scent was not key to their hunting ability. Sweet Lips, Scentwell, and Vulcan were the names of three of Washington's staghounds.

Washington also owned Black and Tan Coonhounds. These dogs were scent hounds, and those whose names are known were called Drunkard, Taster, Tippler, and Tipsy (It would be nice to know more about this choice of names!). One source says that Washington bred the Black and Tan Coonhounds with the Staghounds, which may have resulted in Americas first fox hounds.

A Poodle?

My hunt for additional information arose from a conversation with a new neighbor and friend. Kathy is the owner of a beautiful standard poodle, and when she heard that I was writing about American dogs during the "Dog Days of Summer," she mentioned: "A friend told me that George Washington had a poodle named Pilot."

With that, I was off to research Washington's dogs. Of course, I looked for leads on the Internet and found a few, but nothing on Pilot or any sort of poodle at Mount Vernon. Next, I turned to Ron Chernow's exhaustive biography on Washington to look for more information but came up with no additional leads. Chernow includes some mention of Washington's love of hunting and the dogs he used for it, but there was no mention of Pilot or a poodle.

As any writer/researcher knows, once you have a question in your head, you keep looking for answers. Fate brought me back to poodles when I was researching Dogs for Defense (the war dog program started in 1942), because this canine defense program was started by a woman who bred poodles. This brought me in contact with Emily Cain, a dedicated researcher and writer, who runs the Poodle History Project, a truly exhaustive website with information on poodles.

After connecting with her about information about Dogs for Defense, I asked by e-mail: "Did George Washington have a poodle?" Emily wrote back with a link to the page on her site dedicated to "Companions to Genius." George Washington is one among many people mentioned, and there are direct quotes from his diaries about Pilot, his "water dog" (another name for poodle at the time).

So Washington DID have a poodle. After ordering a reprint of George Washington's journal where Pilot is mentioned, I was able to read about Pilot's exploits. Pilot seemed to be present for many duck hunts, and Pilot must have left a lot of offspring, as Washington's diary indicate that Pilot was a very busy fellow.

KATE KELLY

A DOG ON THE BATTLEFIELD
AND THE CHARACTER OF
GEORGE WASHINGTON

There is no better way to reveal a story of a man's character than by hearing how he treats dogs...here's just such a story about the man who was to become our first President.

The Battle of Germantown

In July of 1777 British General William Howe started moving his forces toward Philadelphia in an effort to seize the city that was serving as the revolutionary capital. Washington and the Continental Army had suffered a couple of serious defeats in September of 1777, and then Cornwallis successfully marched into Philadelphia and claimed it for the British, so American spirits were low. General Howe arranged for the next move for the British, and he sent of his men off to Germantown.

With winter approaching, Washington felt he had time for one more attack, and with the British forces spreading out, Washington thought his men might be able to overtake those at the garrison in Germantown. While Washington's plan was a brave one—and if successful, it could have made a huge difference in the war. However, Washington did not accomplish his goal. He over-estimated his men's preparedness, and the plan, which required coordination among spread-out units, was plagued by incredibly foggy weather.

The men could not coordinate their movements because they could not see what was happening on the battlefield. The British were again successful, assuring that Philadelphia would remain in British hands for the remainder of the war.

Small Dog Found

After the battle, a small dog was found on the battlefield, and when the Americans capture the dog, they saw from his collar that he belonged to General Howe. Washington's men wanted to hold the dog in retribution for their defeat at the hands of Howe's men.

Washington saw the situation from a different view, and he arranged for a messenger to return the dog to Howe with a two-line letter: "General Washington's compliments to General Howe, does himself the pleasure to return [to] him a Dog, which accidentally fell into his hands, and by the inscription on the Collar appears to belong to General Howe."

While many of the stories about Washington's character seem to have been created by his earliest biographer, Parson Weems, this lovely story of kindness and gallantry is one that can be fully documented as a draft of the note still exists. It is written in the handwriting of Washington's aide-de-camp

Alexander Hamilton, and the note can be found in the Washington Papers at the Library of Congress.

KATE KELLY

ABOUT THE AUTHOR

Kate Kelly is the successful author of *You Lucky Dog!* and more than 30 nonfiction titles. She is a contributing blog writer to The Huffington Post, and recently returned to her love of history with her America Comes Alive website and monthly eLetter, American Snapshots. She is an engaging speaker, and has appeared on Good Morning America, World News Tonight, The View, CBS Early Show, CNN and MSNBC.

RESOURCES

PART ONE

Gaslamp Museum where Bum sits:
http://www.sandiego.org/members/museums/gaslamp-museum-at-the-william-heath-davis-house.aspx

I, Toto: The Autobiography of Terry, the Dog Who Was Toto by Willard Carroll
http://www.goodreads.com/book/show/921026.I_Toto

Hollywood Dog Training School
http://americacomesalive.com/2012/08/01/the-hollywood-dog-training-school-a-2012-visit/

Owney and the Postal Museum in Washington DC
http://www.postalmuseum.si.edu/exhibits/2c1f_owney.html

Mike Walling site
U.S. Coast Guard Mascots
http://www.uscg.mil/history/uscghist/mascots.asp

Books by Mike Walling, including a book on Sinbad
http://www.mikewalling.com/books/

Montana School for the Deaf and Blind

http://msdb.mt.gov/

Rin-Tin-Tin: The Movie Star by Ann Elwood
http://rintintinthefirst.wordpress.com/2011/09/29/rin-tin-tin-as-a-puppy-3/

Horatio's Drive
http://www.pbs.org/horatio/

11th Volunteer Infantry, Pennsylvania—Stone Sentinels at Gettysburg
http://www.gettysburg.stonesentinels.com/PA/11Pa.php

Guffey, Colorado
http://www.guffeycolorado.com/

Monster MySpace page
http://www.myspace.com/17480474/photos/45317332

PART TWO

Presidential Pet Museum
http://www.presidentialpetmuseum.com/whitehousepets-1.htm

Millie's Book
http://www.goodreads.com/book/show/997423.Millie_s_Book

Barney videos on YouTube

http://www.youtube.com/watch?v=jc1Q7JuKWYk

William Wegman's Weimeraner, "The Spelling Lesson"
http://www.wegmanworld.com/splash.html

Fala at The Presidential Library and Museum
http://www.fdrlibrary.marist.edu/education/resources/bi
o_fala.html

The Poodle History Project
http://www.poodlehistory.org/

Visit www.americacomesalive.com
and sign up for the regular mailings about America's dogs.

KATE KELLY